Sound
Starters

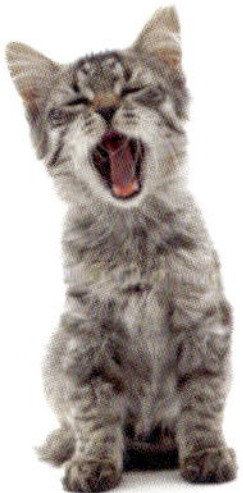

Written by
Stephen Rickard

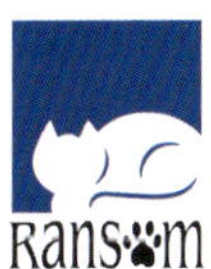

Ransom

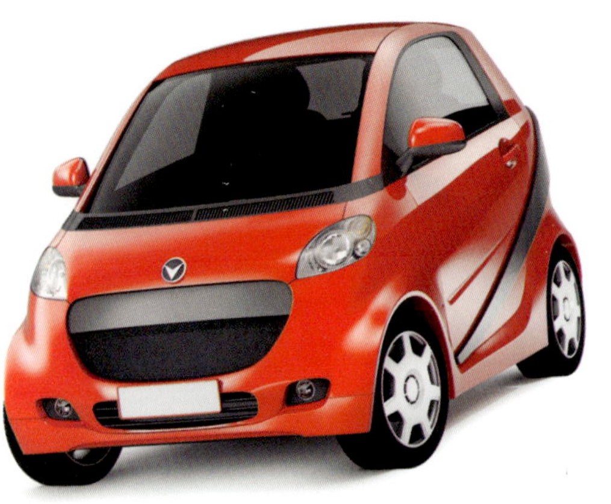

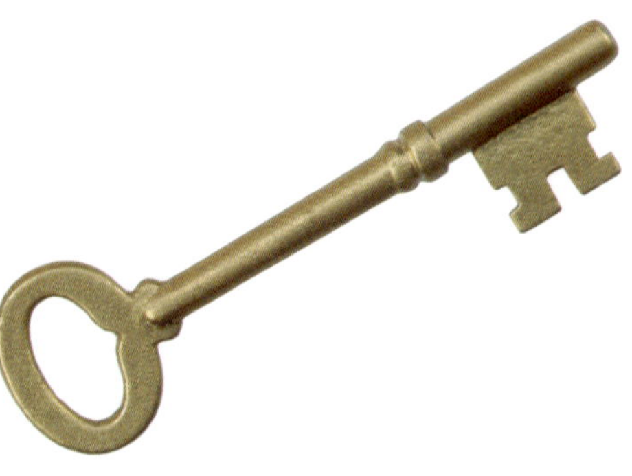

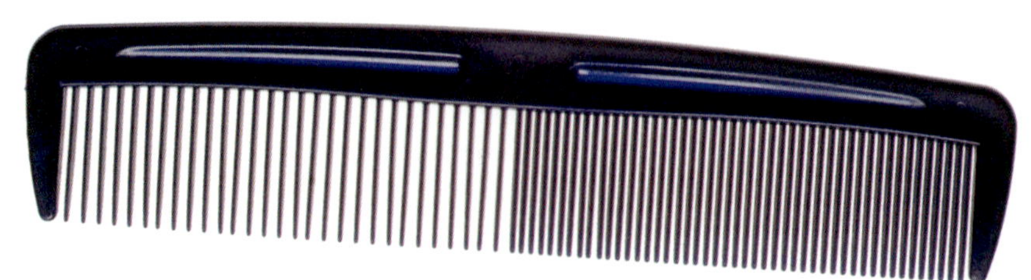

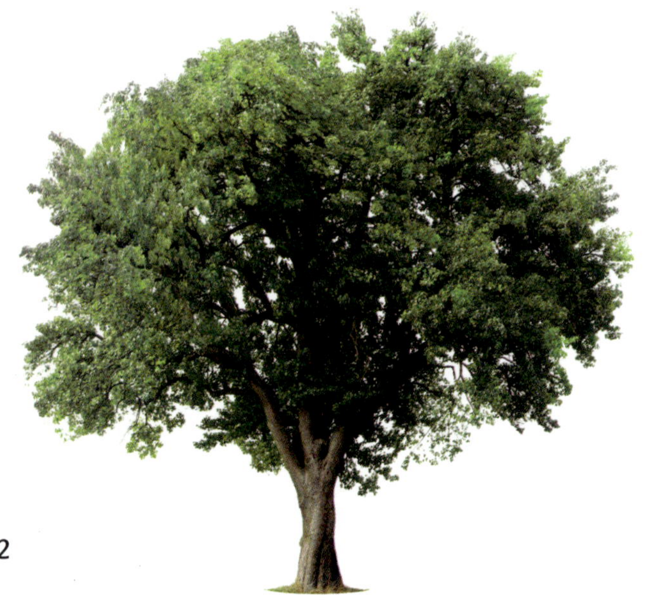

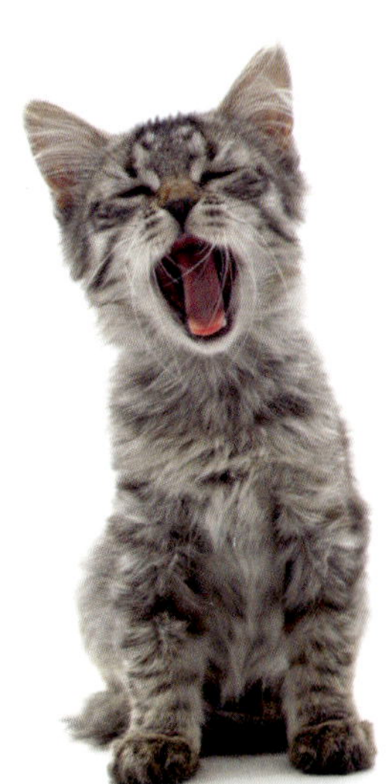

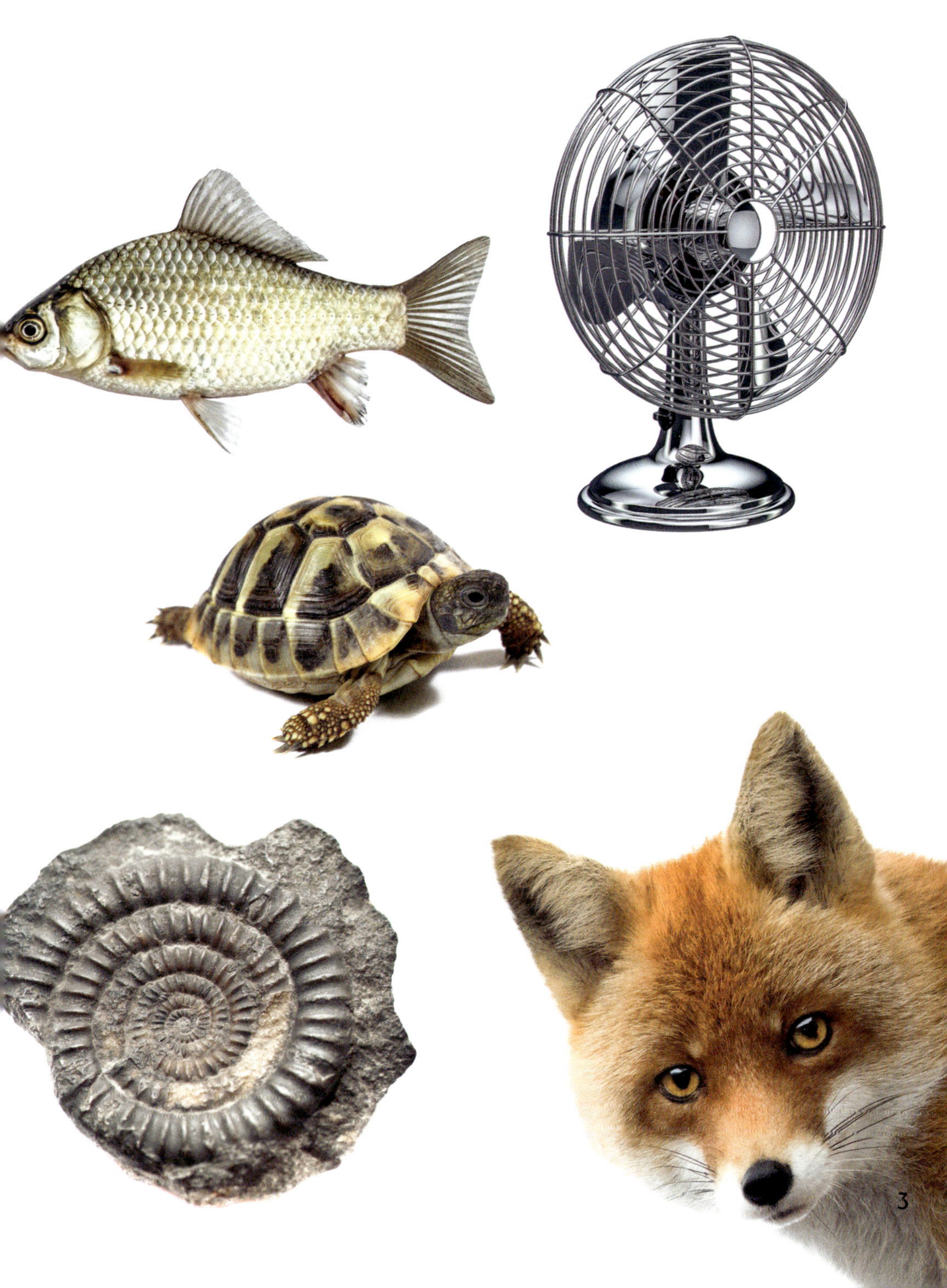

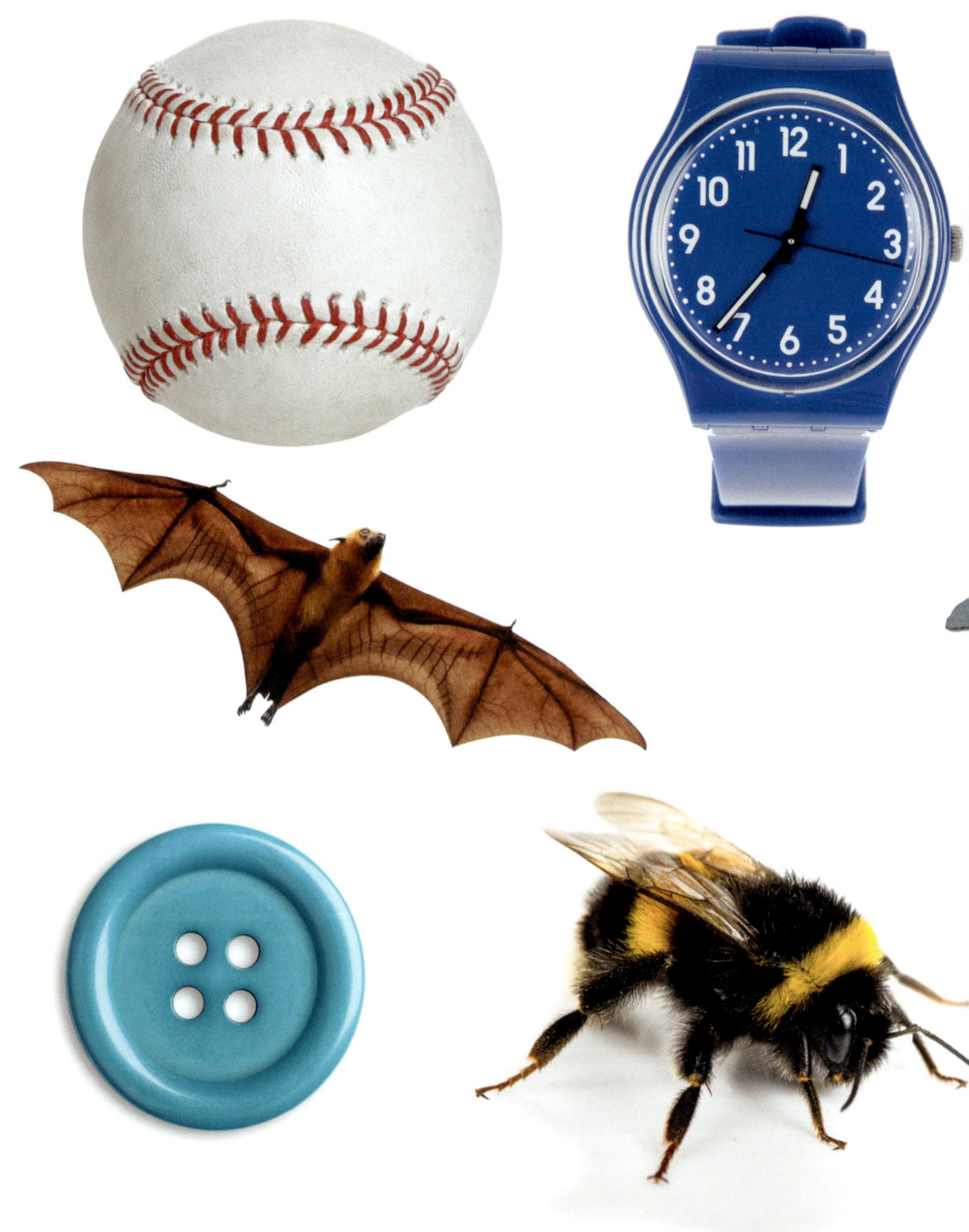

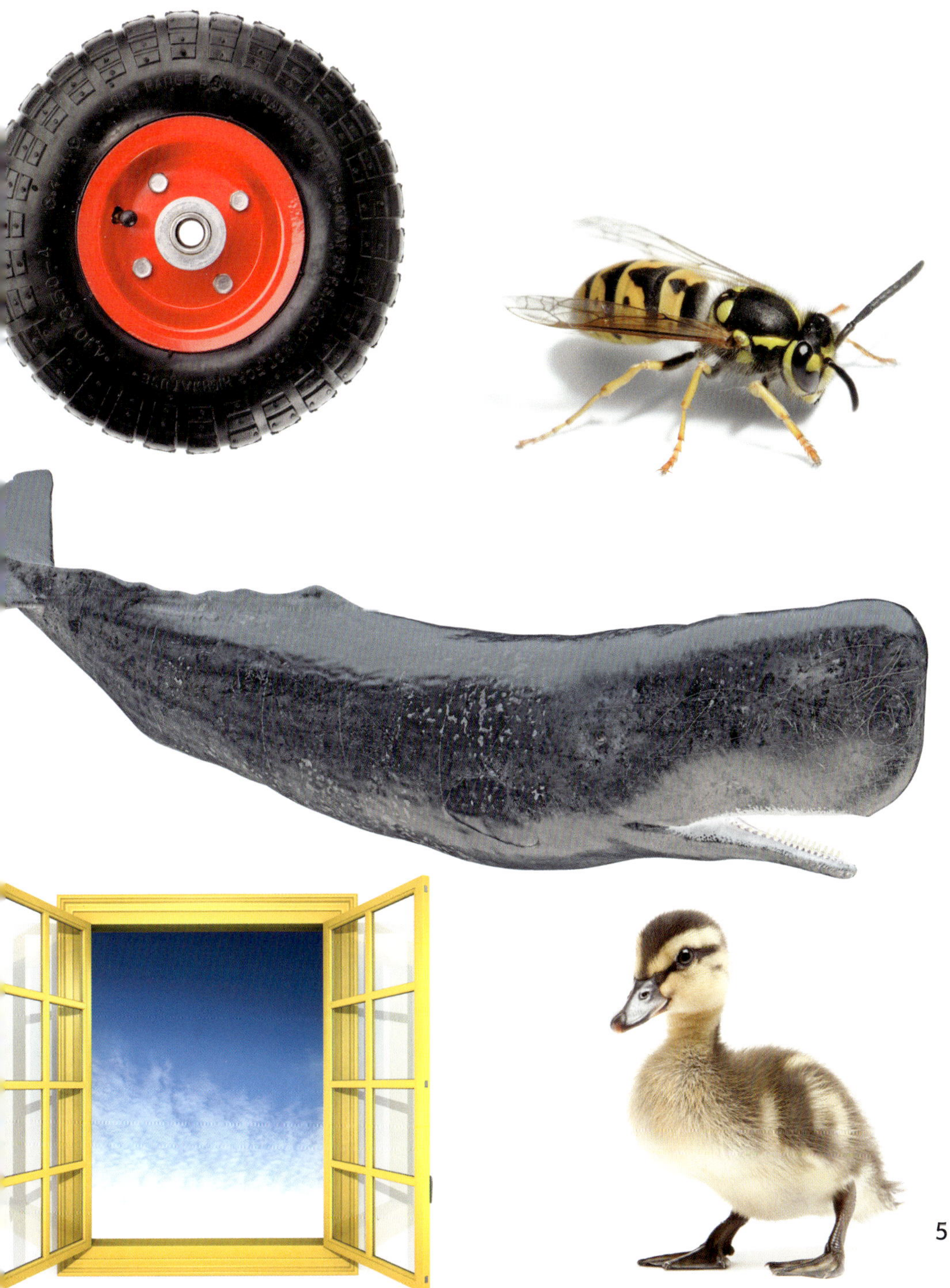

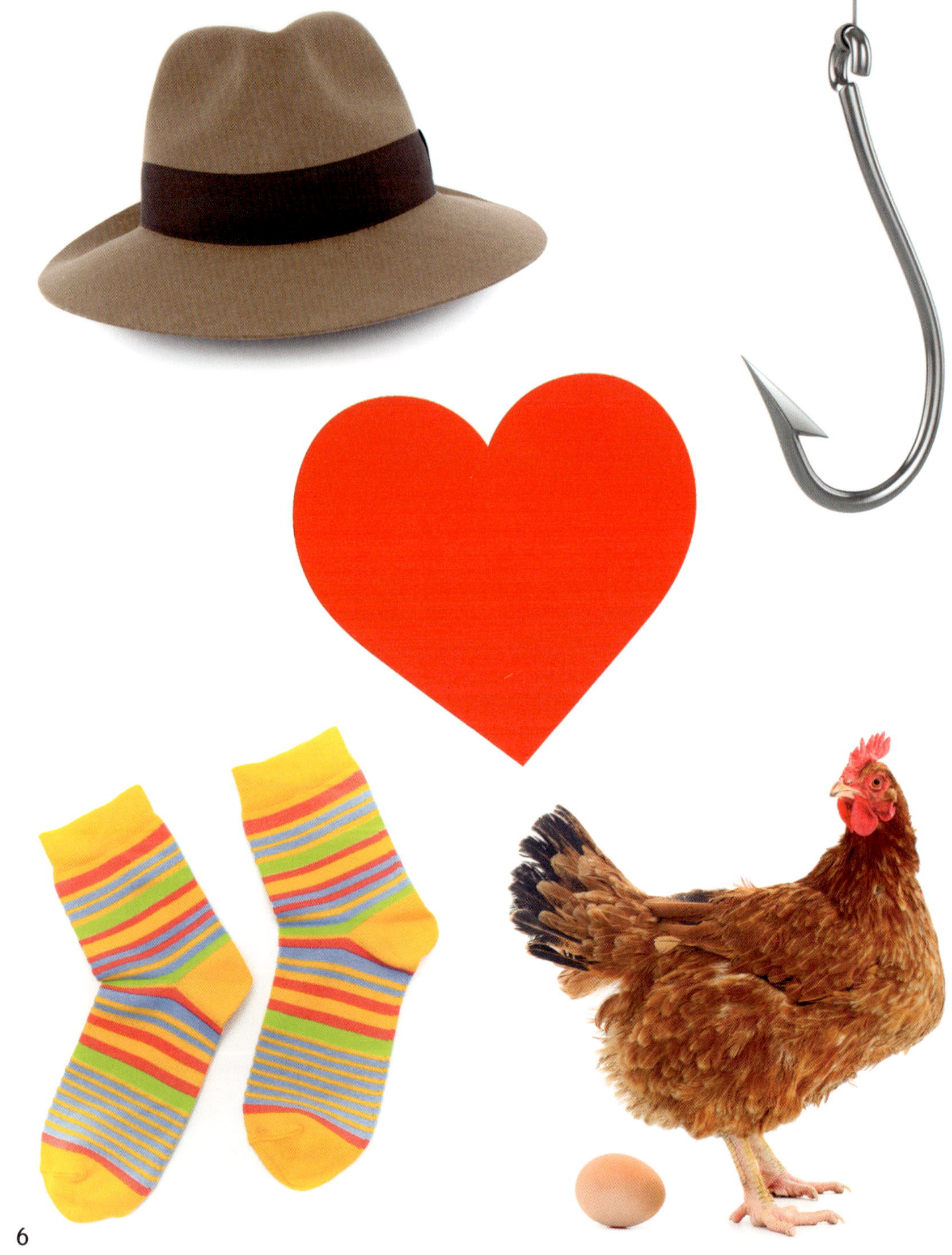

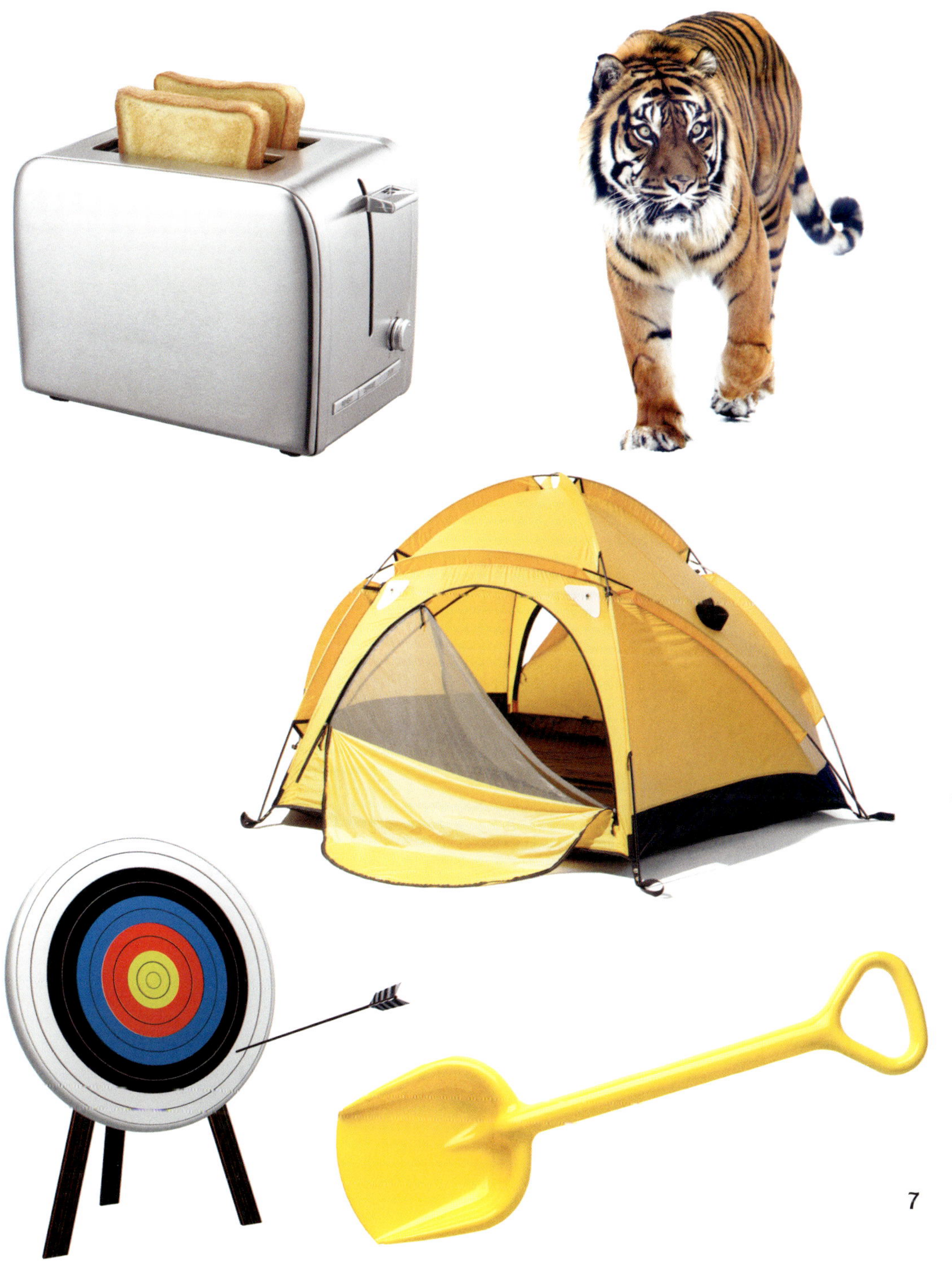

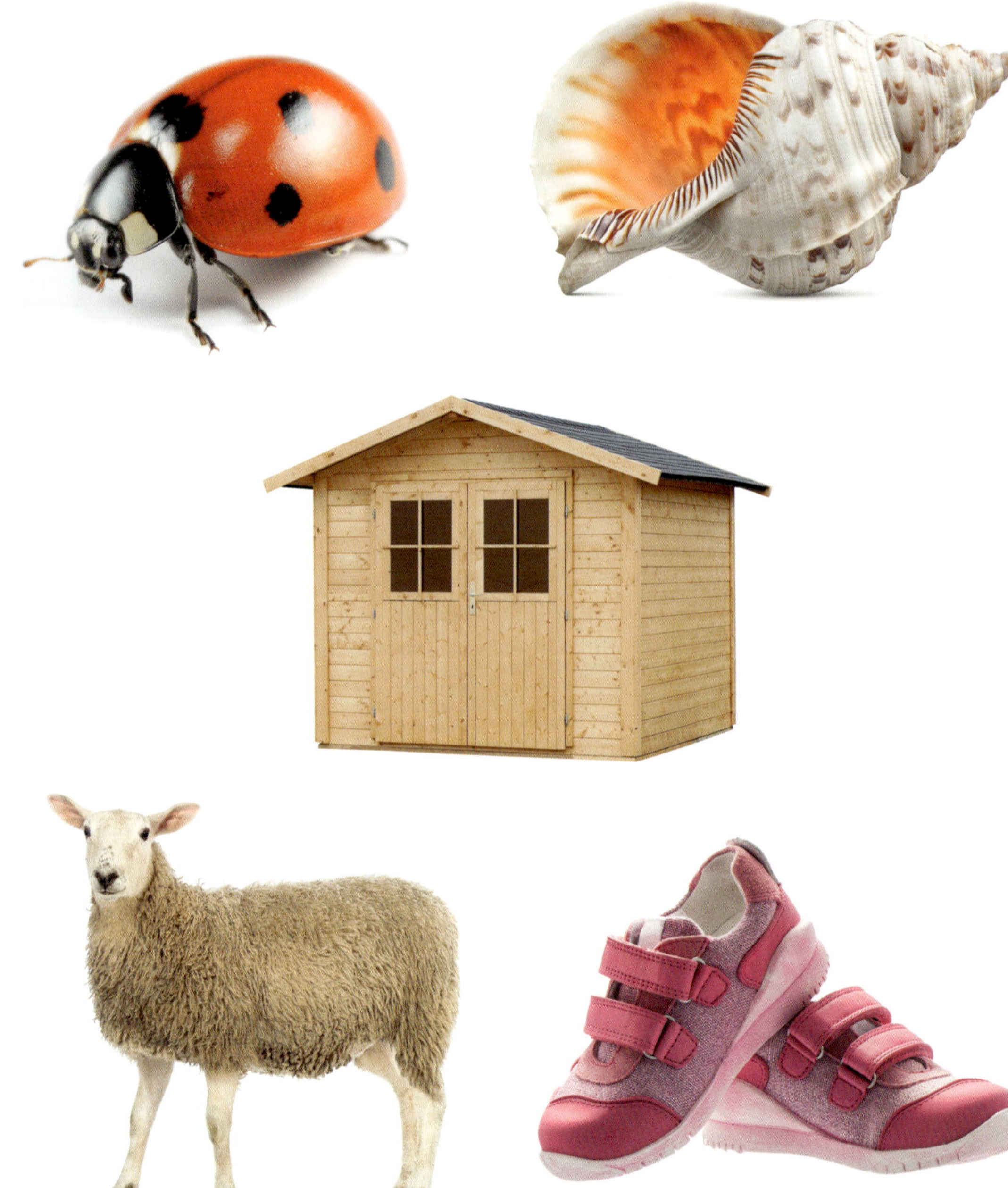